SIMPLE GOD

SIMPLE GOD

by

Robert Hash

Simple God: Six Simple Concepts We Should All Know About God.
Print ISBN: 978-0-9911374-0-4
iBook ISBN: 978-0-9911374-1-1
Copyright ©2013 by Robert Hash

RobertHash.org // SimpleGodBook.com

Book cover by Zech Nelson
zechnelson.com

*To all of those who helped
me find the life I was born to live*

Robert has compiled the *simple* truths of God's Word that has set him free and empowered him to help others. This book is a beginning in discipleship for someone to know and discover *"the life they were born to live"*

–Sharon Daugherty
Founding Pastor of Victory Christian Center, Tulsa OK.

In **Simple God**, Robert Hash shares profound insights that show us how powerful and loving God is! Robert's revelation, of a God who is so simple anyone can understand His love for them, is amazing! Give this book to your friends who need to experience a fresh, relevant God in their lives!

–Jere Peterson
President & Founder of Jere Peterson Ministries

The clear and personal writing style of Robert Hash in **Simple God** lays out the simple, yet powerful, life changing truths about God and the believer. An understanding of these truths is foundational and vital to living the victorious and fruitful Christian life.

–Sandy Kennedy
Pastor of Faith Community Church of Great Bend, Kansas

I have had the pleasure and privilege of knowing Robert for 3 years. He is young but do not be misled! He has a love for God and a depth of compassion for the lost I have seldom seen in anyone of any age. This book is a result of his strong desire to make God understood and accessible to everyone. The TRUE Gospel is *simple* and this book will help anyone have a better understanding of it.

–Mary Rhea McMullen
Founder of Defining Moment Ministries, INC.

This is a good read for those just starting to walk with The Lord and those who've been at it for a while. The simplicity of the truth is so revealing and refreshing.

–Josh Sowiak
Worship Pastor of Harvest Church
Founder of Epic Love Ministries.

In a world where the image of God has been hijacked by cultural interpretation, it is crucial for us to get back to the unchanging truth of who God is. *Simple God* is a breath of fresh air and a must read for all Christians. It encourages and reminds us of the intimate relationship God desires to have with each and every one of us.

–Lucas Cherry
Author of "Not Open"
Speaker for Frontline Family Ministries

Robert never ceases to amaze me with his knowledge and understanding of the scriptures and of the gospel as a whole. His book, *Simple God*, is no exception to what I have come to know about thin and I believe that anyone who comes in contact with this book is going to see this the same way I do. His practical, yet profound, insight is bound to rock you theological world and radically transform the way you see God. God is a good god and this book is a great book. I highly recommend this book for anyone who needs a fresh dosage of the raw truth or an organic gospel.

–Thomas Vigil
Founder of World Love Japan

Many times, due past experiences or unfortunate events, a person's view of God can become very distorted from the Father of love and hope which He is. As I read through *Simple God,* Robert's heart began to quickly shine brightly with intentions to expose this false view of who God is and why He is actually the author of grace and not pain. Through Robert's easy to read layout and self examining questions, I believe you will be wiser to the devil's plot to lure you from the knowledge of God's love while being more empowered to live vibrantly in the plans of God which are initiated by His love to begin with.

–Danny Reed
Senior Pastor of Cornerstone Church, Vidalia LA.

What Robert has done with Simple God is marvelous! He has distilled the characteristics of the one true God into several poignant, meaningful doses of blessings. Both believers and unbelievers alike will receive fresh revelation about who Jesus Christ is, and who He wants to be in their life.

–Dr. Kevin Wagner
Founder of Wagner Ministries International

Robert Hash does a wonderful job of giving us a simple, yet helpful perspective of God and His nature. *Simple God* addresses the real questions we have when it come to living in relationship with God.

–Mark Kresge
Young Adults Pastor of Victory Christian Center

ACKNOWLEDGMENTS

Thank you to all four of my parents, to whom this book would not have been possible. You have been more than I could ever ask for. I love you.

Thank you to all of my grandparents who have poured your love into my life, as well as your patience and forgiveness throughout my lifetime. You are irreplaceable.

Thank you to Pastors Paul and Ashley Daugherty for being my pastors, my mentors, and my friends. Thank you for your trust, your character, and your love.

Thank you to Pastors Danny and Calley Reed for finding me in one of the most difficult times and helping me stay strong in my walk in Christ.

Thank you Ron McIntosh for leading, in excellence, what has helped me find the life I was born to live.

Thank you Zech Nelson for doing everything you do in excellence. You have shown me what a selfless friendship is like and have boosted my confidence far beyond anything or anyone else.

Thank you to Mary Rhea and Laura McMullen. Your wisdom and friendship have made me who I am.

Thank you to Jesus who has dealt with me, built me up, and pushed me beyond who I could be on my own.

CONTENTS

About the Author   13

Forward by Paul Daugherty   15

Introduction   17

Let Us Thank Him For Our Food   20

Seven Billion Favorites   31

Head Over Hands   42

The Rules Rule?   52

Badges for the New Guy   64

Dynamite   75

Conclusion   85

Endnotes   87

ABOUT THE AUTHOR

Robert Hash was born and raised in Natchez, Mississippi. His parents, divorcing in 1995 and remarrying a few years later to amazing people, raised him to the best of their knowledge and are those which he is proud to claim as his own – all four of them.

On June 15, 2005, in Zachary Louisiana, Rob gave his heart to Jesus and accepted Him as his Lord and Savior. Although heavily involved and dedicated to his position in church, Rob didn't understand how much God truly loved him and the extent of God's grace working in his life until later.

After serving for several years trying to earn God's freedom and identity, Rob grew tired of church and went out on his own. After a few months of living in the world, he knew he was called to a higher standard and came back to God. Although shame and condemnation kept him from jumping right back into church, he set his heart to seek God.

In April of 2010, Rob went on a road trip to a youth rally in Georgia. While there, he experienced an empowerment, a new fire, a boldness like never before. On the way back to Mississippi, driving through Birmingham, Alabama, Rob experienced the Baptism of the Holy Spirit and has never been the same since.

After spending a year in Natchez, playing in a small band and serving in the local church again, Rob moved to Tulsa, Oklahoma to attend Victory Bible Institute, now Victory Bible College, through Victory Christian Center. After graduating the two year bible school and a few mission trips, Rob decided to serve in Oaxaca, Mexico at the Roca Blanca Mission Base.

He served there for 5 months, attending the Spanish language school as well as serving on the multimedia team. He took part in medical missions, event planning, and even set up a small computer lab for the on-campus elementary school.

Now, he is back in Tulsa, Oklahoma serving on staff at Victory Christian Center under Pastor Sharon Daugherty and Pastors Paul and Ashley Daugherty.

FORWARD

I have known Rob Hash ever since he moved to Tulsa in June of 2011 and I have seen the transformation of what God has done in his life since. This book is powerful because someone who has been transformed by the *simplicity* of the Gospel wrote it. I met Robert when he was confused, searching, and wondering if God's love was big enough to change his past and give him a bright hope for the future. He discovered how God, in all of His awesome, infinite power, cares about the very details of our lives and desires to show us Himself in a raw, relevant way which can change the coldest of hearts.

God is not a far off cosmic personality, impossible to connect with, or even understand. God is real. And best of all, God is love. He is the ultimate definition for love because HE created it. He is the author of all things good and

He wants us to experience His goodness in every way possible! As Robert highlights scriptures and stories from the Bible that reveal the character and nature of God, you will start to see how the powerful presence of God is *simply* focused on LOVING YOU! God wants that real relationship with you.

When Rob started to grasp the concept of God's love and how his love compels us to embrace love and give it back to Him, there was a change in his lifestyle. So many people focus on changing their lifestyle before they truly have experienced a revelation of God's love for them just as they are. It is the rescuing power of God's love that sees us in our sin, reaches out to us in the middle of it, and puts us back on firm ground to walk out His love. Robert was rescued to rescue–the truth is, all of us are. We have been found by God and invited to experience Him in a whole new way!

My challenge to you is this: read this book and let your heart and mind be open, without pre-conceived ideas about God or even about the author. Be open to discover the new things God wants to show you about Himself. Take notes for each chapter. Journal your thoughts about what God is speaking to you through the pages of this book! It's time to see beyond all the assumptions about God and start seeing Him for who he truly is- *Simply God*. Get ready for a fresh perspective and a new passion to fill your heart as you seek Him through this book!

Pastor Paul Daugherty
Lead Pastor of Victory Christian Center
Tulsa, Oklahoma

INTRODUCTION

I was staying with some friends in Tulsa before I moved to Mexico. Fresh out of bed and quite hungry, I fumbled down the stairs and into the kitchen. After staring into the refrigerator, debating what would become my breakfast, I grabbed the milk. After finding the silverware drawer and a bowl, I went to the pantry to find some cereal.

As I opened the door of the pantry, I saw the cereal boxes on the top shelf, but they were all healthy brands. Every box marked with the mantra of promises and freshness guaranteed. Like any 22 year old young adult, I stared at them for a moment wishing there was something better tasting. Something I would not have to feel obligated to cover in sugar before I could be pleased with its taste. I reached up and shuffled the boxes around to see if there was anything else to choose from. All of a sudden, I got a glimpse into glory! Peering from behind the boxes of wheats and oats I saw the green and orange rings of Apple Jacks®, one of my childhood favorites! I had a hunch there was something other than just the dreaded tasteless cereal.

You may be wondering, *why is he ranting about cereal right now?*, but this illustrates how many people feel about Christianity, even many believers. We may see many beneficial advertisements, wonderful bumper stickers, or cheesy lanyards, but once we commit, the promises seemed slow to become reality. This is why I have written this book. I have been in a place where I hated being a Christian. I was stuck in a system of obligations which continuously beat me over the head with regrets and self-condemnation, even self-hatred.

S. J. Hill makes a profound statement in his book, *Enjoying God*. It reads:

"Jesus never calls us to a life of religious misery".[1]

There are diverse beliefs floating around in the church keeping us at a distance from God; therefore, we need to understand how God has called us into a life-giving relationship with Him. Throughout the pages set before you, I pray the Holy Spirit will bring clarity on who God is, what He has done, what He does now, and who you are in Him[2]. I do not know everything by any means, but what I do know, I want to relay to you. Not only do I pray for you to receive more knowledge, but I pray that the Holy Spirit will speak to you, equip you, and encourage you to live a life of loving God and loving people.

"JESUS NEVER CALLS US TO A LIFE OF RELIGIOUS MISERY".

"Holy Spirit, You are the Teacher. Teach."
- Pastor Bruce Edwards -

As you read, please join our online chapter discussions found at

SimpleGodBook.com

LET US THANK HIM FOR OUR FOOD

- GOD IS GOOD -

It is always amazingly cute when I see one of my precious nieces or nephews bless their food. On one occasion, I visited my sister and arrived just in time to hear them bless the food. All in unison, my two nieces and two nephews prayed, *"God is great. God is good. Let us thank Him for our food. By His hands we are fed. Give us, Lord, our daily bread. Amen."*[1] What uncle wouldn't be proud to hear this?!

Like I said, it is always cute to hear children pray together and I love the uninhibited faith of a child; however, we aren't children forever.

Growing up in the south, I always heard how God is good and I know all of the Christian cliches we put on lanyards and necklaces about God being good; however, throughout life I must continually ask myself if I really believe He is good. I prayed this same prayer I heard my nephews and nieces pray but as life happens and circumstances arise, this is where the everyday challenge comes in.

~

Has anyone ever talked negatively about someone you knew or someone you were very close to? When someone talks about my family or friends, it feels as if they are speaking negatively about me as well. In these moments, it is hard for me to not be offended for that person. Likewise, when people blame something on God or talk irrationally about Him, this same feeling rises up in me because they do not understand how God is a good God. By no means do I know *everything* about God, but as we see in scripture, there are dominant characteristic traits God wants to relay to us.

We, as believers, need to be absolutely convinced of the character and nature of God. Why? Because when someone slanders Him or talks negatively about Him, we won't be swayed and we may have the opportunity to shine truth on the situation. Furthermore, we may simply need to minister to someone. If we know the character of God, we will be equipped to minister in truth. In *God is Not Your Problem*, Pastor Billy Joe Daugherty elaborates:

WE NEED TO ABSOLUTELY CONVINCED OF THE CHARACTER AND NATURE OF GOD.

> *"When you know someone's character or nature, then you can understand their words and actions. When others may misjudge or accuse that person falsely, you can give the accurate picture because you know the true nature of the one being accused.*

God has been falsely accused on many occasions as the one bringing death, destruction, calamity, tragedy, or evil".[2]

The manner in which we see God is so important because the way we see God determines how we encounter Him[3]. For example, if we think God is mad at us, every time something unfortunate or bad happens, we may falsely blame Him or make ourselves think it is from Him. If we think God does not know best, we will not trust Him.

Let us dive into a few portions of scripture which will help us know how God is a good God.

Jesus, God in the flesh, says:

"The thief does not come except to steal, and to kill, and to destroy. I have come that they may have life, and that they may have it more abundantly" (John 10:10 NKJV).

Within this scripture you find so many great pieces of information. Firstly, we see the role of Satan (the thief) and then the role of Jesus, who is speaking. Jesus gives us this portion of scripture to clarify a many things, but let's stick with just two for now:

- Satan's plan to steal. He will try to steal our identity, our blessings, our promises, and our purpose. It is Satan's plan to kill. He will try to bring sicknesses, diseases, and poverty to people. It is Satan's plan to destroy. He wants to bring anything to ruin: people, systems, reputations, and marriages.

- Jesus' plan to bring us abundant life. God wants to bless us! Why? Because He is a good God.

God is good. The devil is bad. God wants to bless us. The devil wants to destroy us. God creates. The devil destroys. God designs. The devil perverts. God heals. The devil kills. God is truth. The devil deceives. I know this seems elementary to go over, but the Body of Christ needs to know this deep down in our *knowers* because if the devil deceives us in understand how good God is, we will believe the works he is doing is from God.

**GOD IS GOOD
THE DEVIL IS BAD.**

~

Here is another aspect of God which worries people about their relationship with Him. They wonder, *is God angry with me?*

Have you ever found yourself thinking God was mad or annoyed with you for some reason or another? It may have been through a feeling of loneliness or guilt. Or maybe you have thought the circumstances which found you were because God may have been angry with you? I know I have entertained the thought and I am telling you now – **God is NOT angry with you!** You may have sinned, cheated, stolen, or you may not even be saved yet, but I say this very passionately: God is NOT angry with you!

Why do I feel passionate about this? Because for years I was trapped in self-condemnation, believing God was enjoying my "godly sorrow". How much did I grow in my walk with Christ then? Not a bit. I lived a defeated life. I never could walk in victory over my life issues.

The truth is this:

"When you were dead in your sins and in the uncircumcision of your flesh, God made you alive with Christ. He forgave us all our sins, having canceled

*the charge of our legal indebtedness, which stood
against us and condemned us; he has **taken it
away**, nailing it to the cross. And having disarmed
the powers and authorities, he made a public specta-
cle of them, triumphing over them by the
cross" (Colossians 2:13-15 NIV).*

Also in Romans 5:8:

*"But God demonstrates His own love toward us, in
that while we were still sinners, Christ died for
us" (NKJV).*

And even Luke 6:35-36:

*"For He is kind to the unthankful and evil. There-
fore be merciful, just as your Father also is merciful"* (NJKV).

Does this sound like an angry God? Both of these
verses deal with God's feelings toward those who have never accepted Jesus as their Savior. How much more does He
love those who have given their lives to Him?

What about people who continue in sin? God brings
correction to them. What type of correction? I'm glad you
asked!

The correction from God comes through the Holy
Spirit who knows all. God **never** uses pain, suffering, dev-
astation, or tragedy to correct.
Satan uses these for his own rea-
sons. The Holy Spirit always corrects us by showing us who we
can be through Jesus Christ and
encourages us to grow. Never
does He condemn us. This brings
us to our next point.

**GOD IS NOT
ANGRY
WITH YOU.**

Who or what condemns people? Is it God?

We can look into John 3 to find the answer to this question. John 3:17-19 declares:

> *"For God did not send His Son into the world to* **condemn** *the world, but that the world through Him might be saved. He who believes in Him is* <u>not condemned</u>*; but he who does not believe is* <u>condemned</u> ***already****, because he has not believed in the name of the only begotten Son of God. And this is the* <u>condemnation</u>*, that the light has come into the world, and men loved darkness rather than light, because their deeds were evil"* (KJV).

The truth is this: all of humanity is condemned by sin; therefore, the Father sent His Son, Jesus, into the world to deliver people from the condemnation of sin. Would a bad, mean, or angry God even want to do this? No! God is a good God. This is why He redeemed us.

HUMANITY IS CONDEMNED BY SIN, NOT GOD.

~

I once visited a great friend of mine. As she, her husband, and I were talking about God's plans for our lives she made a remark which caught me completely off guard. Talking about her daughter, she asked:

"What if God's plan for the man she marries is to die and leave her alone with their children?"

It opened my eyes to see there are probably thousands, maybe hundreds of thousands, of people who are saved yet don't firmly believe God has good plans for their lives, which He does.

God has good plans in store for us! Pastor Paul Daugherty asks this question and elaborates:

> *"What is God's will for my life? Is it God's will that I be sick or impoverish, for my family be angry with each other, or that we live defeated lives? No! God's will is for me to have a good life, for me to not only to be blessed, but to be a blessing".[3]*

What about when bad things do happen? Well, we have to know God's will is **not** always done. I know this is a big pill to swallow, but let me explain:

God has a will, Satan has a will, and we have a will. Our will must be submitted to either God or Satan because that is the only way either of them can work. Sin, whether it was Adam's, ours, or someone else's, influences how events unfold. Just because something happens does **not** mean it was God's will; however, when bad events happen, God can and will use events by turning them around and working everything out for good. These events are not caused by God. They are caused by sin; but, we can see in Romans 8:28 how "*God causes all things to work together for good to those who love God, to those who are called according to His purpose*" (NASB). God does not cause everything to happen, but He does cause it to work together for everyone's good, because He has called everyone to His purpose.

~

To finish our first chapter, I would like to give you some of the names God has chosen to reveal Himself as throughout the Old Testament. Really, take a second to think about each of them as you read them:

•**Jehovah-Jirah**: The Lord who sees ahead and makes provision.

•**Jehovah-Rapha**: Great physician who heals the physical and emotional needs of His people.

•**Jehovah Shalom**: The Lord, our peace.

•**Jehovah Shammah**: The Lord who is there.

•**El Shaddai**: The all sufficient God who freely gives nourishment and blessing; our sustainer.

•**Jehovah-Tsidkenu**: The Lord who is our righteousness.[4]

Through these, we can see God as our Provider, our Healer, our Peace, our Sufficiency, and our Righteousness who will never leave! These are all good names! Why?! because God is a good God. However, the most important characteristic we need to know about God is this:

"***GOD IS LOVE***" 1 John 4:8.

God deeply desires to be intimately intertwined in your life. You need to know it is **not** His judgment, but His goodness which leads people to Him (Romans 2:4). He cares for you no matter who you are, where you are from, what you look like, smell like, or act like!

When you know God is a good God and He loves us, you trust Him. Even if the devil brings trials into your life. You can trust God's plans. When circumstances arise, relax and know He is working it all out for your good!

~

"True, some of them were unfaithful; but just because they were unfaithful, does that mean God will be unfaithful?"
Romans 3:3 NLT

ELISE THOMPSON

I grew up in the church hearing about how God is good and truly believed with all my heart that He is a good God. Through different experiences, both good and bad, I have come to understand that even more.

A few years after getting married, my husband and I wanted to start having children. We were excited to find out I was pregnant, but became devastated and disappointed when we lost the baby a few weeks later. The grief and pain seemed unbearable at times. I wondered that if God was good why He would allow this to happen to me. I felt very confused and heartbroken, but deep down inside I knew that God was going to work things out.

Through the tears and hard times, I saw Him show me His goodness through His comfort and unexplainable peace. He also used people to show me His goodness as they sent encouraging text, brought over meals, and prayed with me. I began to realize that this wasn't the end.

A year later we got pregnant around the same time, but didn't find out until almost the end of the first trimester. It came as such an exciting surprise. It was as if God was showing us His goodness again by protecting our hearts through the delicate first trimester. Currently, I am 10 weeks away from giving birth to a healthy baby boy!

God is a good God, even in the most painful situations. He's always moving and working. We may not see his goodness in the middle of our situation. Sometimes we don't understand why things happen to us, but we can trust that He loves us and is working everything out for our good.

A FEW QUESTIONS

1. When someone approaches you and asks why did God let something happen, what will you tell them?

_____

_____

_____

_____

_____

_____

_____

_____

2. How do you know God is not mad at you? What scriptures show you this?

_____

_____

_____

_____

_____

_____

_____

3. God has good things planned for you, but what about the bad things which happen? Are they from God? Where are they from?

_____

_____

_____

_____

_____

_____

_____

4. What two names of God stand out to you? Why?

_____

_____

_____

2

SEVEN BILLION FAVORITES

- GOD LOVES PEOPLE -

In June 2013, I went to a mission trip to Peru. While in Lima, our contact, Danny, connected us with a special needs orphanage. We painted several rooms, cleaned up the facility, and played with the children.

My first buddy there, Moises, was 16 years old and confined to a wheelchair. We went to a park near to the orphanage where my friend, Loren, and I pushed him on a circular path for almost three hours singing "lalalala/ lalalala/ lalala/ lalalala" to the tune of Paul Leka's "na na na na na hey hey hey good bye". Moises was having a great time! As soon as we finished the song, he started singing it again.

After our park adventures, we went back to the orphanage and helped the rest of the group finish their projects. As we were telling these beautiful children goodbye, God hit me with something I will never be able to shake. Some of these children would never find a home. They would never contribute to society. Some would never know what it feels like to run, much less talk. I felt the special love God has for them regardless of their disabilities. As this flood of emotion hit me, I had to walk outside and pull myself together—at least until we sat down in the bus where I let it all out. As I remember Sandér, I pray he will only feel the happiness he had as I tickled him. I pray for little Sebastiano because as my friend tried to feed him, he wouldn't eat because he was so happy someone was with him. They were all abandoned by their biological parents, but they were adopted by God. Worthless to the world, beautiful to the Father.

God showed me how much He loved them. The government had no place for them, but now they have a special place in my heart and I know they have a special place in God's heart too.

After we left Lima, we went to the Amazon village-city of Iquitos. We partnered with Abundant Life Ministries and got to know several very special guys. These men were so excited about Jesus, it was almost unreal. However, they had stories behind their passion. As we would soon find out, we were surrounded by ex-pimps, ex-drug addicts, and ex-hitmen. These guys made a huge mark on my life and I will never forget how they beamed because they knew how much God loved them, regardless of their past.

~

I am confident that God absolutely, positively loves people. Not just some people, but *ALL* people. Let's take a stroll through some different areas of scripture and by the end of this chapter you will be convinced God loves people too.

Adam and Eve, the first humans, messed everything up for all humanity. They invited sin into humanity. They handed their authority, given to them by God, over to Satan. For the most part, every problem we have on Earth is their fault ... literally.

GOD ABSOLUTELY LOVES PEOPLE. NOT JUST SOME PEOPLE, BUT ALL PEOPLE.

However, let's take a look at how God handled this situation:

In Genesis 3:15, as God told the serpent the consequences of his actions, God promised Adam, Eve, and all humanity He would send a Redeemer. He said *"And I will put enmity between you and the woman, And between your seed and her **Seed**; He shall bruise your head, And you shall bruise His heel"* NKJV.

The New King James Version, as quoted above, capitalizes *"Seed"* in order to give us a glimpse of who is to come – Jesus. Even in the midst of the largest failure in human history, God is not intimidated, but *promises* the greatest example of love which will ever be shown. He gets Adam and Eve out of the itchy fig leaves, clothes them with animal skins, and teaches Adam how he must work the ground in order to eat. Although God must banish them from the garden to protect them from eating of the Tree of Life, God does not leave them without hope or without vividly showing His love for them.

Even later on, after Cain would kill his brother, God assures Cain, *"'I will give a sevenfold punishment to anyone who kills you.' Then the LORD put a mark on Cain to warn anyone who might try to kill him"* (Genesis 4:15 NLT).

Without understanding how God immensely loves people, protection is a completely irrational consequence for murder! Cain sinned, so God should punish him; however, God chose to protect him. Why? Because God loves people, even if they are in the middle of sin. We must know God loves people, lost or saved.

Jesus tells us in His closing remarks, *"Therefore go and make disciples of all nations"* (Matthew 28:19 NKJV). All nations, all people, all ethnic groups, everybody!

~

I have heard some people wondering if God only wants certain "chosen ones" to be His "elect". Granted, there are a few scriptures which seem to point this direction; however, we see more portions of scripture showing God wants everybody!

2 Peter 3:9 tells us *"The Lord is not slack concerning [His] promise, as some count slackness, but is long suffering toward us, **not willing that any should perish** but that **all should come to repentance"*** (NKJV). Paul, discussing authority and living peaceably, tells Timothy how Jesus *"**desires all men to be saved and to come to the knowledge of the truth"*** (1 Timothy 2:4 NJKV).

I don't believe Peter and Paul slipped up and put "all" rather than "some" in these verses. It is very clear in these scriptures that God wants everybody! Even in John 3:16, we see how God sent Jesus to die for the entire world – everybody. We simply must receive this love.

GOD WANTS EVERYBODY.

I want to take a moment to point something else out. Not only is this love for the whole world as a group, but it is also a personal, intimate love. God loves you, personally. He knows everything about you, personally. This is extremely important to know! It is easy to feel overlooked if we see God's love as a corporate love only and not realize how He has personal plans for us, a personal love for us, and personal moments He wants to share with us!

Take Romans 8:35-39. Look it up and meditate on it, personally. Take the words "us" and "we" and turn them into the personal pronouns "me" and "I" and take this promise, not just corporate, but deep and personal.

Lastly, I want to give some application to this concept of God loving people.

Jesus, in Matthew 22, gives us a profound concept which we must take seriously! Here's the situation:

"... The Pharisees got together. One of them, an expert in the law, tested [Jesus] with this question: 'Teacher, which is the greatest commandment in the Law?'

"Jesus replied: 'Love the Lord your God with all your heart and with all your soul and with all your mind'. This is the first and greatest commandment. And the second is like it: 'Love your neighbor as yourself.' All the Law and the Prophets hang on these two commandments." (Matthew 22:34-40 NIV).

Wow! All of the law and the Prophets hang on us loving God and loving people. Let's think about this in a different way:

When Jesus gives us this verse, you could *possibly* see how we can fully and genuinely love God – by loving people. You may also see how we may genuinely love people – by loving God. When we combine the two greatest laws in Christianity, loving God and loving people, we may see a glimpse of how they work together to fulfill the great commission of reaching **everyone** for Christ.

~

I have never seen God's love so clearly as I did when we went to Peru and simply loved on the special needs orphans. When I serve people, I am showing them God's love, just as Jesus did so many years ago.

I encourage you to love people because we are called to be molded into the character of Jesus, who absolutely loved people. When you see someone who doesn't seem lovable, look through Jesus' eyes and know God has a great love for them, whether anyone else does or not. His love is not based on circumstances, behaviors, status, or sin. He simply loves people.

MEAGAN MCGINTY

Now, I had been on the brink of a revelation of God's love for a while, but what I experienced in 2012 and 2013 caused me to tear down the walls of any and all religion in my life.

I had just started my second year of Bible college. I was doing an amazing work study with an office in my church and I had just started an all-girls connect group, all on top of attending two services I volunteered for every week. It was a busy time for me, but I also needed a job! Through the recommendations of some of my classmates, I decided to apply at a widely-known health food store.

I got the job and quickly realized this was no ordinary grocery store. It was a melting pot for people who felt unaccepted by society. I don't want to go in to too much detail, but basically, *anyone* can fit in there. This provided interesting opportunities for me as I began to befriend my coworkers. I met some of the sweetest, most caring people I have ever met in my entire life. I met other people who believed they could change the world and were actively trying to do so. Granted, it was in different ways than I was used to, but I was inspired nonetheless.

Through these relationships, it was brought up several times how much the church has hurt them. Christians with the best of intentions, seeming condemned my coworkers to hell—most of these accusations based on looks alone. I not only saw this first hand, but I was on the receiving end a few times. One instance in particular, I was told by a "guest" that I would be going to hell for just working there with all of these "freaks". This did not make me happy. Actually, it kind of made me wonder how Jesus would feel about all of this. More importantly, I wondered what could I do about it?

I began to care for my friends and coworkers and came to respect and care for them in a new light. These beautiful people had so much bitterness in their hearts towards the the well-meaning Christians who have judged them so harshly. Could I blame them? I could I even defend my brothers and sisters in Christ who, despite their Christ-like intentions, have been everything but Christ like in their actions? What of them? Would they act this way if they knew how much they were hurting God's creations? Even more importantly, could these so called "freaks" ever see God in a good light after the way they had been treated?

> *"I am confident that God absolutely, positively loves people. Not just some people, but ALL people."*

-Robert Hash, Simple God

Then it hit me, I probably can't change an entire religious group. I can't convince every Christian I know to re-evaluate the way they treat homosexuals. What I can do, however, is treat these wonderful people the way I know my beloved Savior would want me to.

God created all of us equally. We are all His children. We ALL sin. I am not justifying any kind of sin, as sin separates us from God. But I would like to urge all of us to obey the Bible. Jesus *commands* us this way: *"A new command I give you: Love one another. As I have loved you, so you must love one another"* (John 13:34 NIV). I don't think He was referring to us loving only Christians there. If He were, pretty sure that scripture would have said so, but no, instead he commands us to love **one another** as He has loved us.

Through embracing this scripture, I have not only experienced God's love on a new level, I have made some amazing friends who have accepted me into their lives, but so many opportunities have come to talk openly and honestly about Christ. No judgement, no premeditated script about sin, just the love of God being presented through not only my words, but my actions. The gospel in its truest form will always be presented through the love of God.

Even though I was constantly bombarded with ministry opportunities in this season of life through Bible college, connect group, and different church activities, I truly believe the most impact I had for the Kingdom of God was when I went to work, just showing God's love to others in the small things. Never underestimate where you are and who you come in contact with every day. Who is hurting around you?

If God can use me to reach other hurting people right where I am, how much more could He use you?

A FEW QUESTIONS

1. In knowing God loves all people, how does this challenge you as a His child?

_____

_____

_____

_____

_____

_____

_____

2. For you, who would be a challenge to love, whether it be a family member, a different ethnic group, a generation, etc.?

_____

_____

_____

_____

_____

_____

_____

_____

_____

_____

3. How can you help fulfill the great commission?

_____

_____

_____

_____

_____

_____

_____

_____

_____

_____

4. How will you exemplify God's love for people this week?
   Be specific.

   _____

   _____

   _____

   _____

   _____

   _____

   _____

   _____

   _____

5. Did Meagan's testimony challenge you? How?

   _____

   _____

   _____

   _____

   _____

   _____

   _____

   _____

3

HEAD OVER HANDS

- GOD WANTS TO BLESS US -

"Since he did not spare even his own Son but gave him up for us all, won't he also give us everything else?"
Romans 8:32 NLT

~

In August of 2013, my friend, Meagan, was moving into her new house and, since I have a truck, I was asked to help. As we were moving, we passed a few garage sales, so we stopped by to see what they had. Meagan was looking for shelves and a small bedside table. The first three garage sales we stumbled across didn't have anything which fit the description, so we continued the moving process.

Mind you, we stumbled across these garage sales, we were not looking for them.

As we stopped at her old apartment to get a few things, we started talking to a few friends who were there. Chatting in front of their apartment door, Meagan spotted something smushed between the rocks lining a pillar. She walked over and picked a crumpled $5.00 bill out of the rocks. Looking around, she asked if it belonged to anyone and it didn't. It was obviously left for someone else to find. Praise God! But, as you can probably tell, the story doesn't end there.

As we drove toward to her new house, there was another garage sale on the side of the road with a small shelf out in front! I pulled a u-turn and stopped in the middle of the street. I asked Meagan for the $5.00 she had just found and returned, placing the shelf in the back of my truck. As I sat down in the driver seat, I looked at Meagan and said, "I don't want to sound over-spiritual, but that just happened!"

~

God wants to bless you. Knowing this will help you trust Him in every area of your life!. If you don't think God wants to bless you, you may work yourself to exhaustion trying to figure out how to do everything, forgetting about His providing hands—a large portion of this grand movement of Christianity.

Before we go too far down this road, let's clarify a few things. God's provision is **not** a catalyst for selfishness. We are *blessed to be a blessing*[1]. If we neglect this part of the character of God, we will miss out on celebrating His provision in our lives and in the lives of others!

WE ARE BLESSED TO BE A BLESSING.

~

    As we are talking about how God wants to bless us, it is important to know blessings are not always financial. Let us take a look at some ways God can, and has, blessed us.

    Ephesians 1:3 tells us to give *"all praise to God, the Father of our Lord Jesus Christ, who has blessed us with every spiritual blessing in the heavenly realms because we are united with Christ"* NLT.

    God has bless*ed* us. This is in the past perfect tense, meaning this has already been done! Ephesians tells us we have been bless**ed** with *every* spiritual blessing. Why? Because we are united with Christ. Simply being a believer, having accepted Jesus as our Savior, is a blessing in itself. Furthermore, God not only offers an escape from hell with this salvation. As we have seen before, Jesus tells us in John 10:10 how He has come to give us abundant life. What a blessing!!

~

    In the Greek, the verb *"to save"* or σῴζω (*sōzō*) is the word which refers to our salvation. This word *"sōzō"* is defined in a few different ways – *"to save"*, *"to make whole"*, *"to heal"*, and *"to deliver"*. [2]

    As we look at these definitions pertaining to our salvation, we can see a few other ways in which God wants to bless us. We can see how He wants us to experience healing–spiritual, physical, and emotional. He wants us to be delivered–from the works of the devil, demonic influences, sin, and hazardous situations. But God doesn't just stop with our spirit and soul prospering. He wants to take it a step further! 3 John 1:2 says *"Beloved, I pray that in <u>all respects</u> you may prosper and be in good health, just as your soul prospers"* (NASB).

God wants His goodness to be seen in the lives of His children, even in our physical needs. I know this is a touchy subject in some areas of Christianity, and once again, this prosperity is not meant to satisfy inner greed, but to catalyze His Kingdom and simply bless His children. Remember, we are *blessed to be a blessing.*[3]

Let's take a look at a few more instances where God show us how He wants our physical needs to be met. In Matthew 6:26-33, Jesus instructs us:

> *"Look at the birds of the air, that they do not sow, nor reap nor gather into barns, and yet your heavenly Father feeds them. **Are you not worth much more than they?** [27]And who of you by being worried can add a single hour to his life? [28] And why are you worried about clothing? Observe how the lilies of the field grow; they do not toil nor do they spin, [29] yet I say to you that not even Solomon in all his glory clothed himself like one of these. [30] But if God so clothes the grass of the field, which is alive today and tomorrow is thrown into the furnace,will He not much more clothe you? You of little faith! [31] Do not worry then, saying, 'What will we eat?' or 'What will we drink?' or 'What will we wear for clothing?' [32] For the Gentiles eagerly seek all these things; for your heavenly Father knows that you need all these things. [33] **But seek first His kingdom and His righteousness, and all these things will be added to you**"* (NASB).

Look at how beautiful these words from Jesus are. First off, He establishes our worth as children of God. Secondly, Jesus tells us not to worry about our physical needs, and thirdly, He encourages us to trust Him. Why? Because He wants to bless us. As we seek Him, we will be taken care of.

Lastly, we see in Philippians 4:19 how Paul confidently declares *"God will supply all your needs according to His riches in glory in Christ Jesus"* (NASB).

Now let us make note of a few other scriptures. Deuteronomy 8:18 tells us God gives *us* the ability to create wealth. Notice how we are the ones who create it, but He gives us the grace to do it.

Also, He give us the opportunity to give. Remember, we are blessed to be a blessing and giving unlocks the spiritual law of sowing and reaping. (2 Corinthians 9:6, Luke 6:38, Malachi 3:10).

~

I remember a time when I was scared to have more than $300 in my account. I believed God hated money. I gave so much money away because I believed if I had too much, God wouldn't like me. Furthermore, even though I gave, it was at the expense of not paying my obligations. Some may see this as a noble thing, but God calls us to be a good steward of what we have been trusted with.

AS WE SEEK HIM, WE WILL BE TAKEN CARE OF.

In conclusion, God doesn't want us to give all of our finances away so we are constantly "trusting in Him". Solomon tells us how it is an honorable thing to leave an inheritance for our children and their children as well (Pro 13:22).

Remember, the *love* of money, not money, is the root of all evil. How cool would it be to be able to pay a million dollars to sponsor several crusades in different countries, or to finance a church plant or an outreach project around you? Honestly, these things cost money.

I urge you, as your soul prospers, to know God wants to bless you too. "*No good thing does He withhold from those who walk uprightly*" (Psalm 84:11 NASB).

Plant your seeds of love, character, and finances. Then, let God take care of you because He wants to.

JESSE WAGNER

I have seen, very clearly, in my own life how much God desires to bless us. Let me tell you my story.

My family and I have an international evangelism ministry. We travel to third-world countries where many people have had little or no exposure to the Gospel in their entire lives. Our ministry functions completely on the donations of supporters, and we are always endeavoring to raise more funds so we can do more of what God has called us to.

A couple years ago, we were going to take part in some ministry endeavors which would require much more money than we had at the time. We knew God had called us to these different ministry opportunities, but we had no idea how we were going to raise the funds to make it happen. So what did we do? We clung to the promises in God's Word: *He will supply ALL our needs according to His glorious riches in Christ Jesus* (Philippians 4:19); *He will honor those who honor Him* (1 Samuel 2:30); *He will give us good things when we ask Him* (Matthew 7:11).

Around this time, my brothers and I heard of a new game-show on national television called "*The American Bible Challenge*". We were immediately intrigued by the new show and wondered if there was a way for us to get on the show. We did some research and found out the auditions for the show were coming up. Long story short, we tried out for the show and made it! A few weeks later, Game Show Network flew us to Hollywood for a week of competition over something that was near and dear to our hearts—the Bible. The cool thing about this show was that competitors did not play for themselves, but for a charity/ministry of their choice. We chose to play for our ministry, *Wagner Ministries International,* and prayed for God to bless our ministry with the resources we needed to do what He had called us to do. Our team ended up winning the first episode and moved on to the second round with tougher competition. After winning the second episode as well, we found ourselves in the final for a chance to win $140,000.

The championship round would have been nerve wracking for most people, but we had such a peace from the Lord, because we knew even if the Lord didn't provide us with the funds from this game show, it would come in some other way. We knew that our source was God, not any person or organization. In the final showdown, we went face-to-face with a team of three nuns and ended up winning it all! God used that game show to provide for our ministry financially when we needed it.

I learned an extremely valuable lesson from that experience. When God promises something, he will make sure that he fulfills His end of the deal when we fulfill ours. We honored God in our ministry, we had been faithful with what God had given us, and in turn he used His creative genius to help us win $140,000 for the furtherance of His kingdom. Here's what you need to know about God: He is not lacking resources, and He can use any means He wants to bless you. Psalm 50:10 reads, *I own the cattle on a thousand hills.* And my pastor usually adds, "and He owns all the oil underneath the hills too!" Here's the point: God wants to bless you, He is your provider, and He can provide for you in conventional or unconventional ways. Trust in Him to bless you.

A FEW QUESTIONS

1. Do you know if God wants to bless you? Why or why not?

_____

_____

_____

_____

_____

_____

_____

2. Have you received the blessing of salvation? What about healing or deliverance?

_____

_____

_____

_____

_____

_____

_____

_____

3. Looking in the past, what is a story of God's provision in your life?

_____

_____

_____

_____

_____

_____

_____

_____

4. Why would you want to prosper? Would it be to magnify your name or your possessions or His name and His Kingdom? How?

_____

_____

_____

_____

_____

_____

_____

_____

_____

4

THE RULES RULE?

- GOD IS UN/RULY -

I was sitting in the lobby of Victory Christian Center working on my computer when the students of the connected school came over to the café. Since the café is in the lobby, I found myself working in the midst of rambunctious middle schoolers.

One student in particular, possibly an 8th grader, was trying to show off his new-found ability. I'm guessing he had been telling other students how he could backflip off of a wall and this was his prime moment. As he ran up the wall, his foot sank right into it and he fell to the ground leaving a perfect foot-hole in the wall. His friends scattered immediately and when he looked around, I was looking directly at him. He quickly grabbed his bags and would have fled the scene.

"Nope" I called out and patted the spot on the couch next to me. He sat down and began to think of the impending doom.

"I'm going to be suspended, and my mom..." his mind raced to the worst of every possibility. His face was so red and he was obviously scared out of his wits. I could only feel bad for him, but yet couldn't help but have a sympathy laugh.

As his fears escalated and he began to panic, I told him to look me in the eyes and reassured him everything was going to be okay. He brushed me off at first, but I told him to look at me in the eyes again and I repeated myself. This time, I saw a bit of peace come over him. I told him to breathe and I would have to report it, but I would do what I could to take care of him.

Telling him this calmed him down. I asked if he had learned anything from this and he replied, "Don't do stupid stuff". I couldn't help but laugh once again. He understood his actions had consequences but knew I wasn't going to *throw him under the bus*. I found out later how his parents would have to pay to fix the damage, but the principal knew it was an accident and reassured his parents of it also.

Granted, I was working on a project concerning grace as this occurred, so I believe it was a learn/apply moment for me; but, when I caught the little guy red handed, I had a decision to make. Yell at him for damaging my church's property, or react like God has already reacted to my sin and failures–my mo-

"DON'T DO STUPID STUFF".

ments of pure stupidity. Yes, he was going to be held responsible for the mistakes he has made, but we need to see how when we mess up or fail, God is not at the ready to strike us down and shame us publicly.

Have you ever clearly been in the wrong? I know I have and I also know you have too–no matter how much you deny it. We all happen to mess things up from time to time and we fully need to rely on the grace and mercy of God. I hate to break it to you, but we will have to do this for the rest of our lives. This isn't pessimism. It's reality.

With this being said, I believe it is a great comfort to know God is not a fault-finder waiting for us to sin. We wouldn't stand a chance if He was. Therefore, we must realize how God is *un/ruly*. What do I mean?

God is not **as** concerned with us following all of the boundaries of Christianity as much as having a real, life giving relationship with us; however, He doesn't want us to live in sin because *"forgiveness of sin is simply necessary to have intimacy with God"*.[1] He is more focused on us loving Him and us receiving His love than us following all of the rules. We fall in love with Him, *then* we will follow the rules out of our passion rather than obligation, but take note the order of priorities. (John 14:15).

Unfortunately, what many of us, as believers, have done is this: we have fallen into *works*. This is what many call *legalism*. Legalism is religion and religion, even in Christianity, is when we try to gain approval or favor from a deity by *earning* it through works or dedication. Legalism in Christianity is when we try to earn what Jesus has already provided! Ironically, it is usually when we are doing wonderful things for God, but with the wrong motivation. We may be trying to gain righteousness, prove our dedication, or compare ourselves to others, but the scary part is this: most of the time, we don't even know it. This is an example of how the devil deceives people.

The reason legalism and religious mindsets are from Satan is because it creates a distance between us and God. Not only that, it keeps us focused on ourselves, rather than on Jesus. Jesus achieved *everything* by grace and we simply accept it through faith. Our dedication, our achievements, and our works could never measure up to God's standard nor could they help us achieve righteousness with God. It all comes from Jesus and it is all a gift. We are all equal at the cross. We all need Jesus, period.

Also, another reason legalism needs to be addressed is because this is what is mostly advertised to the lost world. Many lost people believe Christianity is another set of rules people need to follow; however, when we let the Holy Spirit convict—and we simply love people—we will spread the gospel like Jesus first intended. The love of God changes people's lives, not the rules. So, rather than pushing our rules onto people, let's begin to love them, regardless of their actions, words, mindsets, or theological perspectives. When people experience rules without love, they are pushed away. When people experience the love of God, we let the Holy Spirit do what He does best—teach, correct, love, and encourage.

THE LOVE OF GOD CHANGES PEOPLE, NOT THE RULES.

~

By saying God is not as concerned with all of the rules, I have opened a can of worms because as believers, there are things we have been called to do. Let's cover some basics:

Love God and Love People

As you have seen in the past chapters, God is good and we can love Him; even more, God loves people and as

55

we love people, we are showing our love for God. These two principles, which hang all of the law and Prophets[2], are what Jesus deemed as the greatest commandments. As we love God, by receiving His love first, we will be able to persevere and run the race He has called us to. Remember, Jesus was asked what the *one* greatest commandment was, but He answered with two. Why? Because neither can stand alone. We could not love God without loving people, nor could we love people without loving God. They work together.

Studying The Word

As we study the Word of God, we are reading the words of the Holy Spirit, written over a 1,500 year span by over 35 authors which agrees with itself on all major themes and events. This book, we call the Bible, contains everything we need in life. This book, containing the very Words and actions of God, shows us the power in our salvation, our authority, and the very will of God for our lives. As we read this book, we grow in our intimacy with God, find our identity, hear the voice of the Holy Spirit, and humble ourselves by being teachable before God.

Giving

Jesus tells to "*Give, and you will receive. Your gift will return to you in full--pressed down, shaken together to make room for more, running over, and poured into your lap. The amount you give will determine the amount you get back*" (Luke 6:38 NLT). Also, in Malachi 3:10 God says, "'*Bring all the tithes into the storehouse <u>so there will be enough food in my Temple</u>. If you do,' says the LORD of Heaven's Armies, 'I will open the windows of heaven for you. I will pour out a blessing so great you won't have enough room to take it in! Try it! Put me to the test*'" (NLT). Even more, Acts 20:35 tells us how "*It is more blessed to give than to receive*" (NKJV). Sowing and reaping, as discussed in chapter 3, is a divine opportunity to be a blessing. It benefits us, it benefits those around us, and it builds the Kingdom of God.

Looking in Mark 2, Jesus tells us *"the Sabbath was made for man, not man for the Sabbath"* (Mark 2:27 NIV). Jesus created an opportunity for us to rest. He did not create man to obey the Sabbath, but He made the Sabbath as a gift to people. Some have argued about when the Sabbath is, but I this is irrelevant to what I believe is the bigger picture. Jesus wants us to take a break every now and then and relax, not from Him, but from all of the tasks and to-do's of life. It is a gift from Him which benefits us, those around us, and the Kingdom of God.

Holiness

Lastly, God calls us to live a holy life. The Apostle Paul writes *"since we have these promises, dear friends, let us purify ourselves from everything that contaminates body and spirit, perfecting holiness out of reverence for God"* (2 Corinthians 7:1 NIV). Let me say it another way to elaborate: Since we have been set apart and shown the love of God, let us get rid of the sinful mindsets we have in order to block the attack of the devil upon our bodies and spirits. Why? Because we love God because He first loved us.

First of all, what is holiness? Holiness is an outer separation <u>to</u> God[3]. It is being called out from old things and being set apart for God. This is usually referring to leaving behind sins or mindsets which simply hold us back from the plans of God. It is being separated from sin and dedicated to God. This may seem like a steep request, but let's see why God calls us to live pure lives.

Philippians 2:15 shows why we should live pure lives: *"become blameless and pure, 'children of God without fault in a warped and crooked generation.' Then you will shine among them like stars in the sky*" (NIV). When we stand out to those around us, they will want to know why we do what we do, thus giving us an opportunity to share the goodness of God with them. When we live contrary to the Word of God, it is hard to tell others about our faith. On the other hand, remember you are human and people can identify with real people with real problems, so don't ever feel like you "blew it" because there is always redemption from Christ's cross. No matter what you have done, God has provided redemption; however, when we live blameless lives, separated from sin, it helps us in our evangelism, in our health, in our relationships, and in our communication with the Holy Spirit.

> **WHEN WE LIVE CONTRARY TO THE WORD OF GOD, IT IS HARD TO TELL OTHERS ABOUT OUR FAITH.**

~

So what rules do we follow to be holy? Let's ask a better question. How can I be holy, and yet avoid legalism?

Trust the Holy Spirit working in you. When we give our lives to Jesus, the Holy Spirit comes alive in us and convicts us of certain things. He lovingly corrects us when we do things we shouldn't and He encourages us to do the thing which benefit Him, us, and those around us. Some people are at different places in their relationship with God and the Holy Spirit may call them to do, or not do, certain things, so never compare your walk with someone else's. This is where we have to trust the Holy Spirit working in us and in others.

As you walk in Christ, the Holy Spirit will teach you and lead you. When we as believers do something wrong, the Holy Spirit convicts us of our righteousness (John 16:8), which is never harmful or condescending. If we feel condemned or shamed, that is a work of ourselves or Satan. The Holy Spirit will encourage you to do things differently, but He will not bring guilt or condemnation. Just like Romans 2 and Jeremiah 33 says, you know in your heart what is right and wrong–the Holy Spirit is at work creating this consciousness–so love God, love people, and let the Holy Spirit lead you.

Also, sin destroys all on its own. It brings death, disease, damage, and destroys anything it can. When we sin, we open the door for Satan to attack our lives and sometimes, harm can even come to those around us. God does not want this for us. He sent Jesus to conquer the power of sin so when we sin, He will forgive our sin and give us grace to overcome it! We simply acknowledge our actions and receive the forgiveness.

When you see His grace at work in your life, you will be able to see the same grace working in other people's lives. You can understand how others do not have everything together, just like you don't have it all together. People

SIN BRINGS DEATH, DISEASE, DAMAGE, AND DESTROYS ANYTHING IT CAN.

have problems and they need to be loved and not chastised for their lack of following the rules. We are all in the process and need love and acceptance. When we draw near to people, as God drew near to us, even in the midst of sin, they will see the heart of God flowing through us.

Lastly, understand how we are not called to holiness so we may live in religious misery, but it is to benefit us (so we can hear the voice of God clearly), to benefit others (to give them an example of the Christian life), and to build the Kingdom of God.

~

He wants us to know His love first, then we can trust the Holy Spirit to lead us into truth and holiness. It is not

God's plan for us to be caught in legalism, but to live in intimacy with Him and trusting the Holy Spirit to guide us.

ANONYMOUS

The year after I graduated High School was one of the worst years of my life. I had lost my scholarship to a prestigious university and I couldn't afford to move out of my parent's house, which desperately needed to happen. My siblings never left me alone at home and mostly treated me as if I was the problem of the house.

I had given my life to Christ as a child and many of my family members used it against me. If I wasn't perfect, I would hear the "hypocrite" word. I eventually grew tired of their comments and also the rules my church implemented on its congregation, so I left. I wanted to find God on my own. In my journey to find God, things only got worse. I found myself with no place to call home, except my parents' house. I bounced around from one friend's couch to another. Finally, there was a break.

I fell in love.

I started seeing a high school friend more that often and something sparked with us. We spent so much time together and eventually found our identities mixed together. The problem? We took things too quickly and we wanted out. We broke up and I went from a fanatical "in-love" young man to a guild-ridden fornicator. Now alone and full of shame, all my other problems now seemed magnified. I knew God had a plan for me, but I still felt hopeless.

I had to make a change. I decided to attend a young adult's ministry in Tulsa called IIID. I had heard about IIID for months but never went. When I did, God spoke to me and showed me how much he loved me.

He put on my heart how he loved me through all of the terrible situations. He showed me how he was with me at every moment and he would not have left me, regardless of what I did. The only way I could respond to this was with surrender. I completely surrendered to God that night and I have been running after Him ever since. I am not living from the "fear of the Lord", which I had heard preached as a child. I am living even more from the love he has shone me because to me, that is the best, never-ending motivation He can ever give me. He loves me, and always will.

A FEW QUESTIONS

1. When anybody, believer or non-believer, sins, how will you react?

_____

_____

_____

_____

_____

_____

2. When you are telling others about Jesus, will you tell of logistics of the Book of Revelation, or arguments of theology, or His love?

_____

_____

_____

_____

_____

3. Have you been so dedicated to serving and "living for God" that you have forgotten His personal love for you? How can you make sure this doesn't happen? Ask God if there are any legalistic ways you may need to notice and leave behind.

_____

_____

_____

_____

_____

_____

_____

_____

_____

_____

4. Why does God show us the majority of His rules?

_____

_____

_____

_____

_____

_____

_____

5

BADGES FOR THE NEW GUY

- GOD GIVES US IDENTITY -

So far in our journey we have covered how God is good, how He loves people, how He wants to bless us, and how He is more about intimacy with us than us falling into legalism and empty religious obligations. Now, let's see who we are and who we are not because we have accepted Jesus as our Savior.

~

In 2011, I moved to Tulsa to attend Victory Bible Institute and also began to work in the Victory Bookstore. Both of these positions required me to have an identification badge with my name and a photo.

About two months after my badge pictures were taken, I went through a "makeover" period where I cut my hair and changed my style of clothes. It was clearly a radical change because the first day I walked in school looking all different, several people came by to compliment my change. Soon, my identification badges became false representations of me. The guy in the picture didn't even look like me! Some would even jokingly ask "Who is this guy?"

This same concept happens when we accept Jesus into our heart. Granted, our outer man isn't changed as quickly as my appearance was, but our spirit becomes brand new immediately. Our old selves become obsolete and a false representation of our new selves.

Tony Cooke, in his book *Grace: The DNA of God,* describes how DNA has two parts, the genotype and the phenotype. The genotype "coding" of DNA and what the DNA actually *is* while the phenotype is the expression of that data. For example, the genotypes are bonds between thymine and adenine bases,or guanine and cytosine bases; but, the phenotype is brown hair and green eyes. Likewise, our understanding of our genotype, or our identity in Christ, will become the way are expressed and observed by others, our phenotype. Not only does Cooke describe God's DNA, but he describes how God himself gives that DNA to us when we accept Christ.

Scripture tells us in Second Corinthians 5:17 that, *"if any [one] be in Christ, he is a new creature: old things are passed away; behold, all things are become new"* (KJV).

Furthermore, Galatians 2:20 also says, *"I have been crucified with Christ and I no longer live, but Christ lives in me. The life I now live in the body, I live by faith in the Son of God, who loved me and gave himself for me"* (NIV).

By these two verses, we can see how we are made different—made **new**. Through salvation, there is a shift of identity and we have been made new creatures in Christ—from the inside out. Many don't know they have really been made new; therefore, it is very helpful to elaborate on who we are not.

"...I NO LONGER LIVE, BUT CHRIST LIVES IN ME..."

WHO YOU ARE NOT

Have you ever heard the Christian adage "*I am a sinner, saved by grace*"? Granted, I understand the reasoning and the logic behind the saying; however, I believe this saying has given us a jaded view of who Jesus has made us to be. As believers, we are not sinners saved by grace because ***we aren't sinners***. We may sin, I get it, but we are not sinners because our very nature has been exchanged for His nature (Colossians 2:11-15, Galatians 2:20). To state that believers are sinners would say the nature of Jesus is sinful, because He gave us His nature at salvation. When said this way, we can see the setback this saying can cause in a believer.

Also, you are not your performance. Over time, many people have related to God through their actions, believing if you have done bad things, you must be a bad person; likewise, if you have done good things, you must be a good person. However, the things we do—past, present, or future—do not impress nor do they intimidate God. Our good works are worthless in trying to persuade God to do something for us (Philippians 3:7-8) as well as our sins don't persuade God to **not** do something (Psalm 103:12, Romans 5:8). Our identity is *not* found in our performance—the good or bad, past, present, or future. We cannot earn our identity. We cannot *un*-earn our identity. It is a gift. If we have accepted Jesus into our heart, we have His identity.

Lastly, you are not who people say you are—yourself or others—unless it agrees with who Jesus has made us to be. One pastor even puts it this way:

> *"You aren't what's been done to you but what Jesus has done for you. You aren't what you do but what Jesus has done. What you do doesn't determine who you are. Rather, who you are in Christ determines what you do".*[1]

WHO YOU ARE

As we begin this part of our journey, I believe it is very important for us to remember how we are saved. "*God saved you by his grace when you believed. And you can't take credit for this; it is a gift from God. Salvation is not a reward for the good things we have done, so none of us can boast about it*" (Ephesians 2:8-9 NLT). Notice, we couldn't earn this. We never could have earned our salvation, our identity, nor anything God has done for us. It is completely on the basis of His love and His grace.

As stated before, God has made us new creatures by **exchanging** *our* old identity for *His* new identity. For example, many of us may feel unqualified to receive blessings of God, but He "*has qualified you to share in the inheritance of the saints in light*" (Colossians 1:12 ESV). Many of us may feel dirty as if we need to be right with God before He will accept us; however, "*God made Christ, who never sinned, to be the offering for our sin, so that we could be made right with God through Christ*" (2 Corinthians 5:21 NLT). We do not become righteous after we

WE, AS BELIEVERS, ARE GIVEN RIGHTEOUSNESS BECAUSE OF WHAT CHRIST HAS DONE.

achieve a certain level of purity, but we are given our righteousness because of what Christ has done.

Let's take a look at another extremely powerful verse:

"But of Him you are in Christ Jesus, who became for us wisdom from God—and righteousness and sanctification and redemption" 1 Corinthians 1:30 NKJV).

Jesus is our wisdom, our righteousness, our sanctification, and our redemption

Let's look at righteousness. In Sunday School, I heard how God sees me through the blood of Jesus, but in my heart I didn't believe it. I still had my problems I needed to stop doing in order for me to be righteous; however, in 2 Corinthians 5:21, the Apostle Paul tells us *"God made Christ, who never sinned, to be the offering for our sin, so that we could be made right with God through Christ"* (NLT).

As mentioned earlier, we are not sinners saved by grace, we are the righteousness of God in Christ Jesus. We have exchanged the old nature for the new nature! What else does this new nature entail? Well, Romans 8 gives us two more keys to our identity.

*"And if **children**, then heirs; heirs of God, and **joint-heirs** with Christ"* (Romans 8:17 KJV).

*"We are **more than conquerors** through him that loved us"* (Romans 8:37 KJV).

Even more, Ephesians 2:10 shows how we are an original masterpiece. We, as believers, are the **light** of the world and the **salt** of the earth (Matthew 5:13-16). Honestly, there are so many more aspects of this identity Christ has given us, but let's look at two more:

*"And ye are **complete** in him, which is the head of all principality and power"* Colossians 2:10 (KJV).

and

*"As he **is**, so are we in this world"* 1 John 4:17 (KJV).

Wow. Take a second, put this book down, and think about it. You are complete in Jesus, and as Jesus **is**, so are we in this world! Is. Present tense. Now. That is a lot! God has given us so much. He has taken our old identity and given us His identity! He even attaches us onto the identity of His Son, Jesus! This is insane! As Jesus **is**, so are we in this world. Really, put this book down and think about that for a minute or two.

~

God has given us this new identity because He loves us. The only proper response to this glorious gift, packaged in this great salvation, is thankfulness. When we look at who we would be without Him and who He has made us to be, it is simply humbling. We were given this, not because we earned it, but because He loves us.

Sometimes, however, it is easy for us to feel incomplete in Him. When circumstances arise or we begin to doubt this new identity, questions come up, feelings arise, and ultimately we have a decision to make: Will I be convinced by my feelings, by the circumstances, or by the reactions of others, or will I be convinced by the Word of God? We cannot trust our feelings because they change. Circumstances change. People change. The Word of God is always constant and always true. Even if everything looks contrary to the Word, the Word

THE ONLY RESPONSE TO THIS GLORIOUS GIFT, PACKAGED IN THIS GREAT SALVATION, IS THANKFULNESS.

is true.

What if the facts show you still mess up some-times– or all the time? What if you still do the same things you did before you were saved? Simply, you are living contrary to your new nature and have not renewed your mind to your new identity. We must renew our minds to the truths of our identity because when we begin to see ourselves the way God sees us, we will be empowered to do what God said we can do! Imagine yourself walking in the freedom Christ has purchased for you. Renew your mind to your new identity in Him and you will see it happen.

Granted, this renewal of the mind is not an event, but a process. It is constantly taking your thoughts captive and letting the Holy Spirit show you what is next in the renewal process. Don't ever thing this is a moment, but it is a process that will never end.

Knowledge of your identity unlocks selflessness. Confidence in your new identity frees you to change from self-focused to others-focused. Knowing you are complete in Him and trusting He will always take care of you allows you to be a servant to others in humility, and to show the love of God.

Every believer has been made a minister of reconciliation (2 Corinthians 5:18). We are called to tell people how God is good, He loves people, He wants to bless us, He wants to know us deeply, and He offers a brand new identity to all who trust in Him.

~

"For you are a chosen people. You are royal priests, a holy nation, God's very own possession. As a result, you can show others the goodness of God, for he called you out of the darkness into his wonderful light"

2 Peter 2:9 NLT

JOSHUA FREEMAN

From 2012 to 2014, I was spending time in Haiti doing mission work. Over the course of time, we begin to realize how it's not enough just to lead people to Christ, but to educate them in who Christ is and explain the fullness of the Gospel. So we begin to plan Bible schools in 2013. When we planted our second Bible school, I was asked to be the director of our first Bible school. We had about 120 students come every Saturday so when I was asked to be the director of this Bible school, I couldn't even give an answer. I just stood there and thought about it in two ways: one, this is a great opportunity and, two, who am I to even do such a thing? How can I speak to these students?

I accepted, but I was overcome with fear, anxiety, & stress because I didn't know what to say or what to do. I had been to Bible college a few years before but I didn't feel qualified to direct a bible school. I didn't feel like I knew what I was doing. How could I lead these people into understanding who Christ is? Even for me, I have a difficult time with many things. For example, when I was younger, I struggled to read. The devil would whisper to me, *"how can someone who can't even read lead people? How can someone who grew up in a neighborhood like you did even think he has something important to say to anyone."*

I began to forget who I was in Christ and all the things he had pulled me out of. God had given me so much but yet I had forgotten. I forgot the new identity and the new mind he offers to us. When Saturday came, it was time for me to teach. As I'm standing before them, I look out and I see 120 students waiting to hear the Word of God.

The only thing I can think of is this: to pray. I asked God to come into the situation and in the middle of my prayer, God reassured me how He had called me when I was young He had chosen me and, just like in the book of Jeremiah, He had anointed my lips with the words to preach.

He reminded me how it was him through me. He reminded me how he made me sufficient and in my weakness, He made me strong. I realized that Christ has made us all the same *in Him*: we are all brothers and sisters. When come together, we can continue to empower each other in him and to show the world how they too can be changed from the inside out by what He has done.

A FEW QUESTIONS

1. Are you a sinner saved by grace? Explain your answer.

_____

_____

_____

_____

_____

_____

_____

2. Is your identity based on your performance or Christ's
   performance? How does this change your perspective?

_____

_____

_____

_____

_____

3. How did you obtain this new identity?

_____

_____

_____

_____

_____

_____

_____

4. What two aspects of your identity in Christ stand out to you personally?

_____

_____

_____

_____

_____

_____

_____

5. What are you going to do with your new identity in Christ?

_____

_____

_____

_____

6

DYNAMITE

- WE ARE POWERFUL -

"But you will receive power when the Holy Spirit has come upon you; and you shall be My witnesses both in Jerusalem, and in all Judea and Samaria,2 and even to the remotest part of the earth"

Acts 1:8 NASB

~

In the summer of 2013, I was staying with friends before I moved to Mexico. Halfway through my stay, they went on a vacation and left me in charge of the house. They gave me the keys and a few things to do. They asked me to water the plants, take out the garbage, and enjoy myself.

They left me in charge of what they had purchased, they delegated the keys to me, and they told me to take care of what was theirs; likewise, Jesus has purchased salvation on the cross, given us identity, and now, we will see how we have even more than salvation and a new identity.

So many believers don't know they have been delegated the very authority of Jesus. This creates a problem. We may go from one person to another trying to use their dedication or devotion to God and neglect our own authority. For example, I may be praying for my Uncle Fred to be healed of cancer. Since my prayer is seemingly unanswered, I ask Mrs. Sally to pray for him because her prayer would be more convincing to God. Don't get me wrong, there is power when people agree in prayer (Matthew 18:19-20), but when we try to use someone else's dedication to do what Jesus has enabled us to do, a problem is created.

Even more, some people want the pastor or one of the church leaders to pray for their family members, believing ministers have more of an advantage; however, the Apostle Paul tells us all of the church ministries were given in order to equip the *saints*.

You do not have to be in a recognized church leadership position to be a minister. The job of the church leaders are to equip the *saints* for the work of the ministry (Ephesians 4:11). Furthermore, *all* believers are called to be *ministers of reconciliation* (2 Corinthians 5:18). You, as a believer, are a minister of the gospel of Jesus. Does this mean you should quit what you are doing and become a pastor or a leader in the church. It might, but let's look at it this way.

Jesus said "*Go into all of the world*" (Mark 16:15). Slightly elaborating this commission, Oral Roberts built a university under the premise of sending believers into "*every man's world*" with the gospel[1]. Oral Roberts felt as if it would be more strategic to put Christian *influencers* in government environments, in the science and research fields, in the classrooms, and throughout the business world as opposed to simply having church leaders everywhere. As the ministry of the pastors, teachers, evangelists, prophets, and apostles equip them, the saints are given the opportunity to go into their own environment with the gospel of Jesus' love and be the missionary they have been equipped to be.

"GO INTO EVERY MAN'S WORLD".

What I want you to do now, in order, is this: finish this sentence, fold the corner of this page down to keep your place, put the book down, look at your hands, and say "Jesus wants to use these hands". Do it, now.

MY HANDS

It is so important to know you are a dangerous weapon against Satan. Colossians 2 shows how Satan is a defeated enemy. He still has not been destroyed, but he has been defeated. When Jesus died and rose again, He gave believers the authority to enforce Satan's defeat. In Mark 16, Jesus lists a few signs which will follow believers–two of which are casting out demons and healing the sick. Both of these are offensive against the kingdom of darkness. God has blessed every believer with His authority because we have the Holy Spirit living on the inside of us.

To recap, Jesus said *we* can do even greater things than He, and just as He is, so are we in this world (1 John 4:19, John 14:12). We have been empowered by the Holy Spirit to lay hands on people and see them healed. We have been empowered by the Holy Spirit to enforce the defeat of Satan in our daily lives. We have been empowered to live as more than conquerors through this salvation by His grace which we have accepted through faith.

As we have seen in earlier chapters, God has a will, Satan has a will, you have a will, and others have a will. God is a gentleman. Satan is a brute. You have a choice if you will yield to God or to Satan. God will honor your will and partner with you to build His Kingdom. Satan deceives us and if we give him an inch, he will take a mile, yet still using you. Sometimes, this may happen and you never realize it; however, when we resist the devil, he flees from us (James 4:7).

You have the choice to build your own kingdom, to build God's Kingdom, or to build Satan's kingdom. It is ultimately your decision.

~

Lastly, before we close out, I want to add a few things about authority. We have been given authority from Jesus to build, further, and enforce His Kingdom on the earth. In Luke 10, Jesus sends out 70 of His followers. These 70 followers were never recorded to have names, but we see how Jesus gave them authority to cast out demons and to heal the sick.

All of this, as Jesus explained, was not to build people's pride, but to show the goodness of God and further the gospel. Nothing confirms the power of the gospel like a good, old-fashioned miracle.

~

In July 2013, during the One-Nation-One-Day campaign in Honduras, one lady heard our team creating commotion in a nearby school. She heard about other school services we had done in the area and quickly brought her step-father and her daughter to receive prayer.

In this beautiful moment, we prayed together and made Jesus the Lord of their lives.

As we finished praying, I knew there was more. I asked the lady if she had any pain in her body, to which she replied yes and patted her shoulder. I hadn't noticed until now how her arm wasn't very mobile and she kept it close to her stomach. I cupped my hands on her shoulder firmly and, through my broken Spanish, commanded the pain to leave and for healing to come. As I said "amen" I looked into her eyes and asked her to do something she couldn't before. She first started to roll her shoulder around. I noticed discomfort in her face, so we prayed again. After this, she began to cry as she started to freely move her arm. It was her own special miracle.

I turned and asked the gentleman if he had any pain in his body, to which he replied yes. He simply told me his knees hurt. I couldn't tell but I wasn't going to discount his faith. We prayed and afterwards, he was bending his knees and raising them all the way to his chest. I couldn't tell if he was in pain to begin with, but I know a genuine smile when I see one and there was no denying this. In the past twenty minutes, this gentleman received Christ as his Savior and then received healing in his knees!

During all of this, I didn't have chill bumps. There wasn't any over-spiritualized music playing in the background. It mildly shocked me, if I can be honest. Shouldn't I *feel* God working so strongly? It may have been the language barrier or maybe I am not so spiritual, but I saw my authority in Christ working to show the heart of God to other people. It was never about me. It was about God's love for them.

Some would think this authority may create pride; however, when you have moments like these, it just doesn't seem fair. I *was* a sinner, but then God saved me. I *was* a nobody, but then He made me somebody. I *was* just little ole me, but He chose me and there cannot be anything more humbling.

This same authority I have seen work through me is alive and active inside of every believer—*inside* of you. Simply believe and do something. You have the Holy Spirit *inside* of you. You have the authority of Christ. You have been qualified and empowered to take part in the miracle working authority by the love of Jesus.

God has anointed you to be a minister of the gospel of reconciliation and when you walk in this calling, no matter your occupation, position, or qualifications you will "find the life you were born to live".[2]

DANIEL WAGNER

When Rob asked me to write this testimony, I admit to being somewhat intimidated. I admit I do not always feel like an authority on the subject of the miraculous.

Growing up, my dad was involved in full-time evangelism, traveling overseas and holding large open-air meetings. Every trip to India, Pakistan, the Philippines, or Rwanda was full of salvations and, yes, miracles. As a 13 year-old, I began to travel with my dad and have since been overseas more than a dozen times.

We have seen much fruit in our ministry—many, many salvations and many, many miracles of healing and deliverance. When we are overseas, in India, for example, we usually conduct a 3 to 6 night meeting. Each night, our first and primary goal is to see the Lost brought to salvation, which is the single most important thing we can do after our own surrender to Christ; but we have a secondary goal, and it is to see the sick healed, the broken made whole, and the bound set free.

Christ was the epitome of virtue, never sinning once; further, He was *God*. Simply because He calmed angry waters and removed leprosy should not mean we are able to do so as well—right? And yet, it was those stunningly ordinary Apostles—Peter, John, James, Thomas—who were empowered with God's Spirit and brought His healing—both spiritual and physical—wherever they went.

Is Christ less powerful today? Is His healing virtue less needed? Has His desire to set captives free from their bondage to sin and sickness and depression weakened? NO! I have had the immense privilege to see blind eyes opened (literally), deaf ears unstopped (literally), lame legs walking (literally), cancers removed (literally), demons driven out (literally), and more than that.

A few weeks ago from the time I am writing this, my oldest brother, Joshua, was in the island-country of Madagascar for a three-night evangelistic meeting. Allow me to share with you a story from that trip:

On the second night of the crusade a man named Layee came on the stage to testify to a miracle. As he began to speak in his native language the crowd started to cheer wildly! I (Joshua) immediately asked my interpreter what had happened to Layee and she told me, "For four years Layee has been completely deaf in both of his ears. He came to the crusade tonight believing for healing and when you prayed, both of his ears were opened and he can hear perfectly!"

Jesus healed Layee. Why wouldn't He? It's His nature to heal.

I mentioned at the beginning of this testimony that I felt intimidated by Rob's offer to write about my experience with the miraculous power of God. Speaking honestly, it's a difficult subject for me, because I have often prayed for the sick to be healed without results. I am sure of God's sovereignty, and I know He is always good. But there are times of serious frustration for me; I desire so strongly for the power of sickness or disease or sin to be broken in the lives of people. But, many times, I see no physical manifestation of God's power.

And yet, the reality of the matter is that a man named Layee is hearing out of his now-healed ears today. Once again, I state, we've seen in our ministry many, many salvations and many, many miracles of healing and deliverance.

Here, I must address a concern some readers may have: We need to make it powerfully clear that we seek miracles not because of their inherent popularity. We desire to see the miraculous take place because the sick need to be healed, the bound need to be set free, and the broken need to be made whole. Further, we seek the miraculous because Scripture teaches us that The Lord confirms His Word by the signs that accompany it (Mark 16:20), and that the message of the Gospel is enhanced by a "*demonstration of the Spirit's power*" (1 Corinthians 2:4).

Scripture is clear: Christ is the healer, and the miracle-worker. He has empowered His followers (including you and me) with the same supernatural ability with the intention of furthering His Kingdom and restoring what has been broken by sin. He is good all the time, and His Word is incapable of failing.

That is what I know. Here is what we will do: because God responds to our faith, and not our need, we will continue to believe for the miraculous (by God's grace, we will choose to believe every day and in every situation); we, as the church, should continue to pray for healing. And I am confident of this: the Lord will confirm His Word by the signs that accompany it (Mark 16:20).

A FEW QUESTIONS

1. Who did Jesus delegate authority to: only the first century Christians, only ministers, or all believers?

_____

_____

_____

_____

_____

_____

_____

2. What is your occupation? Student? Parent? Business? Medical? Anything. How can you be a minister of the gospel there?

_____

_____

_____

_____

_____

_____

_____

3. Does God's will always get done? Explain your answer.

_____

_____

_____

_____

_____

_____

4. Why has Jesus delegated this authority to us?

_____

_____

_____

_____

_____

CONCLUSION

These are just a few things God has specifically used to show me freedom, to show me peace, and given me the confidence to call myself a Christian. These basic principles can transform the way you walk through your Christian life. So many are living in "religious misery"[1] but this was never God's intent. So take what you have read in these pages and fulfill the Great Commission and live the great commandments.

Love God and Love People

ENDNOTES

- INTRODUCTION -

1. Hill, S. J., Margaret Feinberg, and Mike Bickle. *Enjoying God : experiencing intimacy with the heavenly Father.* Lake Mary, FL: Relevant Books, 2001. Print.

2. Mcintosh, R. 2012. *Organic Christianity.* Shippensburg: Destiny Image, Inc..

- LET US THANK HIM FOR OUR FOOD -

1. Child's Mealtime Blessing.

2. Daugherty, Billy J. *God is not your problem.* Shippensburg, PA: Destiny Image Publishers, 2006. Print.

2. Mcintosh, R. 2012. *Organic Christianity*. Shippensburg: Destiny Image, Inc..

3. Victory.com. n.d.. *Victory.com*. [online] Available at:https://www.victory.com/watch/foundations/2036398578001 [Accessed: 23 Aug 2013].

4. Blueletterbible.org. 1990. *Blue Letter Bible - The Names of God*. [online] Available at: http://www.blueletter-bible.org/study/misc/name_god.cfm [Accessed: 23 Aug 2013].

- HEAD OVER HANDS -

1. Victory.com. n.d.. *Victory.com*. [online] Available at: https://www.victory.com/watch/foundations/2036398578001 [Accessed: 23 Aug 2013].

2. Blueletterbible.org. 1994. *Blue Letter Bible - Lexicon :: G4982*. [online] Available at: http://www.blueletter-bible.org/lang/lexicon/lexicon.cfm?strongs=G4982 [Accessed: 26 Aug 2013].

3. Victory.com. n.d.. *Victory.com*. [online] Available at: https://www.victory.com/watch/foundations/2036398578001 [Accessed: 23 Aug 2013].

- THE RULES RULE? -

1. Mcintosh, R. 2012. *Organic Christianity*. Shippensburg: Destiny Image, Inc.. p26.

2. Matthew 22:40

3. Blueletterbible.org. 1940. *Blue Letter Bible - Dictionaries :: Holiness,+Holy,+Holily*. [online] Available at: http://www.blueletterbible.org/search/Dictionary/viewTopic.cfm?type=getTopic&topic=Holiness,%20Holy,%20Holily&DictList=9 [Accessed: 29 Aug 2013].

- BADGES FOR THE NEW GUY -

1. Driscoll, M. 2013. *Who do you think you are?*. Nashville: Thomas Nelson. p3

- DYNAMITE -

1. Webapps.oru.edu. 2013. *Alumnus of the Year Nomination - Oral Roberts University - A Christian College, based in Tulsa Oklahoma..* [online] Available at: https://webapps.oru.edu/secure/alumniweb/nominateAOY.php [Accessed: 3 Sep 2013].

2. Vbitulsa.com. 2013. *Victory Bible College.* [online] Available at: http://www.vbitulsa.com/ [Accessed: 3 Sep 2013].

- CONCLUSION -

1. Hill, S. J., Margaret Feinberg, and Mike Bickle. *Enjoying God : experiencing intimacy with the heavenly Father.* Lake Mary, FL: Relevant Books, 2001. Print.

If you have enjoyed this,
please visit

ROBERTHASH.ORG

OR

SIMPLEGODBOOK.ORG

to contact us and stay connected.

or mail us at

Simple God Book
13829 River Road
Natchez, MS   39120